FULL DEPTH:

The Raymond Knister Poems

*To Selina,
In all sensual and joyful
inspiration*

FULL DEPTH:

The Raymond Knister Poems

Micheline Maylor May 2017

Micheline Maylor

WOLSAK
& WYNN

Cover image: Micheline Maylor
Cover design: Rachel Rosen
Typeset in Garamond, printed in Canada by The Coach House Printing Company, Toronto, Ontario

Some of these poems, or earlier versions of them, have appeared in: *The Alexandra Reader, The Antigonish Review, Amethyst Review, ARC, CV2, Descant, Equinox UK, Fabric UK, FreeFall, Gaspereau Review, The Harpweaver, Manuscript UK, Pennine Platform UK, Reed USA, Seam UK, Smoke UK,* and *Windsor Review.*

The publishers gratefully acknowledge the support of the Canada Council for the Arts, the Ontario Arts Council, and the Book Publishing Industry Development Program (BPIDIP) for their financial assistance.

ONTARIO ARTS COUNCIL
CONSEIL DES ARTS DE L'ONTARIO

The Canada Council | Le Conseil des Arts
for the Arts | du Canada

Canadian   Patrimoine
Heritage   canadien

The author sincerely thanks the Alberta Foundation for the Arts for its financial assistance and The Leighton Studios at The Banff Centre for their support.

Wolsak and Wynn Publishers Ltd
69 Hughson Street North, Suite 102
Hamilton, Ontario L8R 1G5

Library and Archives Canada Cataloguing in Publication

Maylor, Micheline, 1970-
        Full depth : the Raymond Knister poems / Micheline Maylor.

ISBN 978-1-894987-17-2

1. Knister, Raymond, 1899-1932--Poetry. I. Title.
PS8626.A9328F84 2007   C811'.6   C2007-900310-9

Thanks to W.N. Herbert and my Lancaster class, and Michael Bradford for editing the early drafts. Exceptional thanks to Chris Wiseman, without you this book would not exist. Thanks to Shelley and Ross who made it possible.

Contents

Preface

Raymond Knister, poet and novelist, was a rising star on the Canadian literary sky in the early twentieth century. In August 1932, Ray Knister went out alone on the lake in good weather and calm water with a small boat. He failed to return. His wife's family, as they owned a shipyard, were summoned from Toronto to drag the lake for his body.

Three days later the body washed to shore. The official cause of death was drowning.

I include reference to the rumours of suicide, not to perpetuate the rumours, rather to imagine what a quagmire of emotion his widow would have experienced.

This story is not meant to be a historic account. I do not claim to know the truth. It is a work of impressions. This is my view of their story.

Micheline Maylor

1. Prologue

The field

Across the green mirrored surface
the orchard and the nutmeg sun

her laughter fat as blossoms
peals all the way into the night.

I know she's there
the birds are scattering

though I see nothing
no one but flight.

Dark lady

She raps on the window
when I turn in the drive
the quickening shakes my skin alive.

I must leave lights on to illuminate
dark corners on my journey
from room to room. She shows me

their initials carved in the window frame.
I trespass into their love, hear their secrets,
feel watching eyes. The surface holds their touch.

The lady retreats, her eyes shine
in every doorframe. She whispers her will
then, I inherit their hushing.

Perspectives

Reading this as a story would be easy,
a mystery or a romance.
But I read this in fragments

separate lives scattered
among many sorts of pages
incremental images warped

by the fog of time leaving spaces
to fill with fallible words
truth too slippery to grasp.

2. The rumours

Lake

Charcoal clouds in south Ontario
can roll in faster than gambler's dice
and swallow a man whole.

1932. The grey came like a flame licking at the hard
high wind, and he could not stroke fast enough
despite the burning in his arms from trying.

I am coming home. I will make it home.

Water thicker than dreams, warm as amniotic fluid.
Light filters through the drops now,
falls on the surface pulled tight as trout skin.
Weeds and shrouds bind a man,
all his struggle leaks out into the lake.

He is calm now,
seeing a disaster
from a particular point of view
where nothing can be done but watch.

Widow

Up above the turret, dark chews the weather vane.
She stares into surreal light her belly turns arabesques,
fingers press into the pane.

Come home. It's dark Ray. Raymond, come home.

The curved glass makes her feel on the inside
of a fishbowl. The whole world turns in coloured laps.
She swims. Captured.

Don't you take him. I need him here with me.

Night is coming. A velvet cloak drags across the exhaling sky
falls here on this small lake house.

Imagine

this man walking to the beach.
Sun, an eye in the four o'clock sky,
children on the beach older than his own
calling for daddy
everywhere.

Singleness of purpose.
The knot heavy as knowledge
as he pushes into the late summer water
the lick of it teasing his ankles
pebbles catching in his toes.

He steps into the boat,
the heat of wood seeps into his skin
hot as a kiss from an illicit lover.

Stroking out he scans for holes and weeds,
rolls his clothes over without care, like the pile
on the floor he left for his wife to collect.

Just lean in.

Under the surface he inhales a foreign air
a foetus born, welcomes the slick against all instincts.
He binds his hands in green as he pictures her
wrapped in a forest of silk.

The heap

She stepped around it for days,
the boyish pile of clothes,
as if it might be dangerous
to feel the weight of it.

Pussyfooted, as if
the spill of objects,
trousers, shirt, socks,
could lure him back
from the black womb.

Night comes around again.
The silver belt buckle yawns
at the moon's pocked darkness
mouth gaping
on top of the crumpled heap.

In the wardrobe

She crawls in at 2:14 am
just to be near the scent of him.
The hangers clutch the last of his smells.

Leafing through shirts
she buries her nose into cuffs and collars,
inhales all she can
before the unmerciful air
steals what is left of him.

She shuts the door behind her,
winds the garments around her body
like the weeds that took him away.

Memoriam

Writer, cab-driver, farmer,
father, dreamer, lover.

Drowned under the shimmering skin
of Lake St. Clair at four o'clock in the afternoon.
Just 33 years old.

A most promising career cut short
during a family holiday. Prize-winning
novelist and poet, leaves wife
and daughter, just two years old.

Known for his excellent posture,
his ability to recite Keats, his strong embrace,
his precise right hook, and his love of spiced ham.

There is a sharp drop off the sandbar
where the boat was last seen.

His body not yet recovered.

Among his literary peers
whispers of suicide.

Painting the scene

Daub on a skiff among a sea of blue
two small oars tucked into the prow.

Near the stern a spot of white -
a robe perhaps, tidy as a little room.

To the left, a beach, stone-brown
and on the sand a swirl of colour, a cacophony

of red, yellow, and black. A jumble of
limbs all in motion and stilted
towards the vanishing point.

Beach

Heat will remain in the sand
for hours after the sun sinks.
She knows this still.

Where are you hiding Ray?

Seventh trip to the water's edge
to hear the disappointing slap
slap of waves on the distant rocks.

Night birds call.

How dare you play this trick on me

Eyes skim the horizon, dart behind rocks.
Pale legs flash in the moonlight
bare soles pace over cooling ground.

The ship

Though she was not there to greet the prow,
it must have come near dawn.
She prepared the house when
she could not pace the beach,
dusted his books,
swept the floor, dusted his books.

Waited for three long days
before they hooked him back,
a stiff and bloated mess
decomposing.

Her husband
no more dignified than fish,
naked. Weeds entangled with his limbs.

They kept all this from me.

Do you hear his voice?
Behind the lowing horn,
a whisper song from his blackened lips.

My dearest one,
my dearest one . . .

The lake

Will not apologise for what he's stolen,
for what he's eaten then spit up on the shore.

He'll only yawn at the waxing moon
exhale a little then ask for more.

3. Courting M.

Replacement

Three candles on the table
when I blew in late and flustered.
You handed all the food to me.

Lord, how I knew you were the one
and when I snuck my arm behind you,
in you leaned!

You weren't supposed to come
sudden as a rush of taste.
The replacement and the only one there

who said such things,
Wine? Bread? Brie?

Uncle Jack's veranda

On the wood solid and dark
I wait here while our smoke rises.
Uncle Jack retreats into the cooling walls
his footsteps wane.

Then the night makes a friend of himself
shows me the stars in his throat,
the moon in his palm.
And this is the best thing

since her warm breath slid behind
my ear and I felt the horses in my own blood,
the forge of iron under my skin,
the soft slip of love in my bones.

Storm after ploughing

Dark enough that I can't
make out if my eyes
are open or closed.

Each muscle burns
smithy hot. The windows
gasp open
help cool the embers.

Just before the lightning
brightens the sky
I remember our laughter.

Sketching

You draw me out of charcoal. I try
to set myself in stone but my eyes slide
down the high line of your cheek, the sleek
silhouette of your bones. *Sit still,* you say.

The dark of your hair casts shadows
in your almond eyes. Kiss me.
I want to feel the hot of your lips,
the thin of your shoulders. *Sit still, Ray.*

I slip perspective and let my hands drift down
the fragile buttons of your spine, circle your waist,
pull you towards me. I almost catch the scent
of the sweet nape of your neck, a kiss

drives us both silly. You flick your hair back,
smile at me, set the drawing on the easel,
then arc into a liquid stretch on the chair
lucky enough to hold you.

Lovely day

Her legs tuck under a periwinkle skirt
fabric pants under the press of heat
long fingers caress my ear.

Clover weaves patterns onto her legs
where skin touches the earth. I trace
the shoreline of her eyes, her cheeks

rise to meet the tide that grows
from those patient black centre points.
She's waited for me, for this reflection

all her life,
all my life.

The Charleston

Our kitchen window lights your face
from one side as the sun yawns
towards the shadow time of day.

Cinnamon smeared on your apron, a smudge
behind your ear, the smell of crisp apples
on the counter top. I take your hand

and everything about your skin excites me.
It's hot in here and I am dissolving
like rock-candy. Shrinking,

so small, as the scent of everything
is stirred by your dancing legs. I swirl
with them, evaporating

until I am only pint-sized
when the phonograph stops.
I land,

tiny as a sugar grain,
a minute speck,
sticky on your neck.

When I wake

I wake to lavender. Yes, this is the scent of you.
The colour of lilacs,
but not the white ones. No.
The purple ones.
Light of the morning filters through too much glass
makes the hedge shimmy with colour.
Your lashes catch on the splits in my rough lips.
The mornings you slept.
My senses ran about your body.

Garden tomatoes

Nipped off the vine, segmented
I like them with salt

dipped into granules of white
juicy, red, seasoned with summer

so much like your lips
and me begging to taste

just one more delicious piece.

4. M.

Spiced ham

My love for you is
simple as my purple thumbs
pressing into cloves.

Simple as waking you up from some
ever-after sleep with the aroma
of unfinished love.

Parlour

Mother would leave us alone
if she could hear the phonograph.
So I sketched while he
set the record spinning.

He caressed my shoulders
above jewel-blue fabric
loving the melody
and all those tiny buttons.

He blew poems like waves along
my neck. I imagined the sun-hot beach
we played song after song
each accompanied by a tremble

coming from inside, the way the frames
of the pictures rattle with the passing trains.

Barn

Into the night, the air is thick
with cricket sounds,
mayflies landing everywhere.

Through the dark we wade. You are holding
my hand. I try to keep my mouth closed.
You make me laugh. A line then, from Keats,

Then felt I like some watcher of the skies

splinters of moon fall through the beams
light snags on a million strands of hay.
You whisper another poem and I open
myself to the golden flow of words penetrating
the softness. The universe is split
wider than the deep great lakes.

My palms

Red as fever after he drove.
Always shouting and gesticulating
at the scenery, hitch-hikers, anything.

He'd lose his stammer talking to me
or driving. He'd go on about destiny,
howl loud as that old Ford.

Flail like a flame in the wind.
He never once noted my clenched
fingers on the door wanting to bail.

Accidents

are always so loud in the city.
So loud when children fall.

Why was yours quieter than kisses Ray?
You must have slipped over the boat

into a ripple, missed the edge of the sandbar
fallen into the hole where the cold water waits

full of clams and fishes. Mute witnesses
to a new type of marine life suckling

the lake into yourself, binding
weeds to the slow blueing of your skin.

There was no storm as some may say.
Just the calm, the sun, and the silence

of my panic and the colour of
my mouth stretched into a scream.

Eclipse

1. *The total or partial obscuring of one celestial body by another.*

   He was swimming beside the boat. His head just visible. I took my eyes away.

2. *The period of time during which such a phenomenon occurs.*

   For just one moment.

3. *Any dimming or obstruction of light.*

   I rushed into the water and yelled through my hands.

4. *To cast a shadow upon; darken; obscure.*

   Fat as an omen that moon
   walked in front of the sun
   while we were searching.

The red sweater

It lay on the beach when those boys
brought me back after searching.

We searched until our skin stung with sun,
until the boat was out of gas,

There it was, Ray.
That panic-coloured thing.

It had the courtesy you did not.
It waited for me.

Reconsidering

The moment you left
remains an indelible stain.

The babe slept peacefully
as you stepped into your trunks.

I stayed when you left. Then,
having thought better of it. I woke her.

We ran to the beach, to try
to catch you before you rowed away.

We yelled after you but you didn't hear.
You had water, dark as ink, in your ears.

The very next day

With nerve I have yet to earn she sent me
a letter before his body was found.

Dear Mrs. Knister, would it be possible
For me to gather Ray's poems into a collection . . .

His body had not even been recovered
This is the way it was with her.

Those men in boat and planes still looking,
my tears long stopped falling,

just dry weeping
not staining her fresh, fresh ink.

The body

Bloated, blood-clot black
ripped from a twisted root
then washed ashore like driftwood
naked there for the crowd.

Such contrast on the brown sand
I could see from far away
though someone tried to turn my head.

My Ray. My darling. Stiff
among curious eyes.

I struggle with a familiar yet
unfamiliar man as he steers me away
from your familiar yet
unfamiliar embrace.

The ring

Under the sunlight
the ring glimmered merrily
as the day we were married.

Infinitely.
But we were married finitely
as the sun glimmers in the day,

merry as a holiday beach
before they brought the thing
for me to identify.

Cockeyed

Boys can imagine
near anything.

I suppose it was a pastime
to talk about him
bleakly.

Her, too, imagination bigger
than the darned lake
to insinuate suicide.

My sister threw that cockeyed
memoir
clear across the room.

Sometimes

your voice
pushes into my task
the particular way you say
my name.

Or I'll choose one of your books
with the pencil markings
and I'll hear you say,

Listen to this!
You must hear this passage.

Anniversary

Fifty years after our wedding,
the new people let me into my own house.
Young, smiling cautiously, they smell of earth.

They've changed our kitchen. No more wood stove.
Cowboy wallpaper. Everywhere.
This room has holstered guns.
That one has mounted horses.
The hallway girl looks like Dale Evans.

This is not my house
until I find our initials carved
into the window frame
on the turret stairs.

R loves M

A few names beside I've never seen or known.

Pete '71, Peace J.G., P.K., Mike was here

That day, sixty-some years ago, giggling,
hiding, kissing in the stifling heat, lips sticky
with lemonade. Your hand on my breast.
Then you traced with your finger
our initials on the canvas of my throat.

Make it last, Ray.

Those fingers took all day.

5. Five Meetings

Curiosa

Just like the first day I ever saw you, Dee.
It was almost as clear as today. Do you
remember when we met. Lanky, stammering me
calling at your mother's door, sheaf of blue

pages in hand, asking for help. You were
so lovely, those young fawn eyes writing
your name on my heart; then sitting for
hours you'd read my poems as if singing.

We'd sit on the porch while the trees shook
their leaves and I shuffled my pages.
Sometimes your arm slid into the crook
of mine as we talked and there we stayed for ages.

You were fifteen years old, fresh as an unopened
book, dangerous as little words left unsaid.

Tilling

Steam exhales out of the earth this morning
soil spreads wide, moisture caressing me
my feet push in, furrow down, furrow down

steam exhales out of the earth this morning
the sun on me bigger than your goodnight kiss
my hands blister on the plough, I smile, I smile

steam exhales out of the earth this morning
soil spreads wide, moisture caressing me.

Siren

Not so wise as to have myself tied up
I venture to your door loose
as an unknotted rope of hair.

The fabric of your dress caught
by the wind wraps around my arm.
In this moment I become aware

of a tiny fly near the banister being wound
in silk. Skillfully, quickly, and without hope.
As I enter, you begin to hum a tune.

Cigarette

Clouds low enough to reach,
dark as pressed tin.
The humidity has capped out
all of the good fresh air.

Her hand pulled the pack
as if it were too heavy,
wrist limp under the weight of it,
and her red red lips

Wrapped around the tip.
Her skirt,
her eyes tinted by sea.
She gazed at the molten end,

exhaled slow as lava ash
suspended somewhere in gravity,
falling hot and gentle.

Freckles

It's unseasonably hot
this summer of the silk worm.

Through the day, the sun burrows
and beats my skin Indian red

seems to strip my muscles
as I push and pull the ground

groove a mile of furrow
with the wing of my plough.

As usual, I wait for the shift
to twilight, the blue deepening

into cool then the moths flutter
into the sky, little brown specks

scattering like freckles did
when I leaned in to kiss you that once.

Virtue

Night a silent voyeur
and, God knows, everything in me
alive and on guard, and you

tempting me with skin and breath
your necklace hung gleaming
in the eye-light of the moon as you

pulled all the lovely night-words
and every trick to get me to lay with you,
and though you believed you failed,

I tell you now, it took everything I had
to deny you. Everything
to get into that damn car and drive.

If I were to ask

You'd come to the house leaving
footprints in the snow only halfway
to the door. I'd look at them for hours,
examine the arc of your foot,
the tread of your sole. Then,
I'd be lost remembering the curve
of your leg and the colour of your
bare ankle under the kiss of sunlight.

Will you forgive me now?

For not being home when you finally called,
for ignoring the courage it took for you
to come right up to the door.
For sending her to tell you I was away,
while I hid in a back room and thought
of fingertips caressing the back of my neck
while mumbling aloud, *"that darn girl
what a bother, that darn girl."*

In snow

The scrubs of grass poke their heads
up into the light and ask, why not?

And I do not know what to say.
It happened that I never knew you in snow,

though I would have knelt like a beggar
to shim you out of a drift on a day like today,

to read our future through the wool on your palm.
We'd have made angels, you and I,

under the cold scatterings of cloud.
I could have pushed you down into it,

kissed the melted spray from your cheeks,
given you shelter under the heft of me.

I have no answer for these grains,
for why I never knew you on a frigid day.

But I knew you, Dee. Oh yes.
I knew you in the hot season.

Recurrence

The dream of us, limbs entwined
Out from the abyss again this morning
Into daylight the vivid receded

The dream of us, limbs entwined
Two delicious green long-lived vines
Forever in bloom, forever courting

The dream of us, limbs entwined
Out from the abyss again this morning.

6. Dee

Crush

A warning barked at me through the heat.
Then Ray came. I watched from my window.

Silhouette pressed onto the sun, wearing a Sunday suit.
I felt the heat in those polished shoes.

He read me poems with a voice thick as fluid song,
while I thought of his hands, jungle damp

pressing the air right out of me.
He was the only man

who considered the full depth
of the half full green pitcher and me.

Bluestocking

I knew he could see me over mother's shoulder
getting ready for school. *Dee, don't be late.*
I could sense his gaze hop over to me
and if I turned my head I'd see the lamp
balled like a fist, his straining eyes and I
could hear his thoughts as I rolled those stockings up slow
slow
slow.
Each fingertip alive as though they might be his
and when I paused mid-gam
to smile,
he'd clear his throat,
Ahem.

And I'd go on,
yes, I'd go on and on.

Breathless

He wrote a poem
about my legs.
Softer than new grass
he said.

He read it to me
over the telephone
so that I wouldn't
see him blush.

Then he set down the receiver
and tore the page
slowly into long pieces
as I listened, not moving.

The farmer boy

With the urgency of a growing season
he'd slather me with heat, whip up a storm.

On that night an infestation of June bugs
came to encrust the window screen.

Fourteen species of trees perfumed the air
the night I gave him shelter in the foyer

while his gaze, big as black-eyed Susan's,
burred in deep as memory as we listened

to thousands of beating wings passing
through the night, ephemeral as this life.

The decision

Before I left for Paris
I showed him some poems
knowing I was at the cross-roads.

Dream it deeper, he said.
so I did.
And so it is.

Remembering you in Paris

You called at my mother's house,
polished handsome.
I touched myself after you left,

the scent of you and me
still on the hand you held
as you read me some of your pages.

I lay watching, with closed eyes,
explosions of colours, ripe
as the taste of raspberries.

The accused

The whispers are no worse than one bony
finger pointed straight into my face.

Your wife thinks I am a home wrecker.
but that night in Clarkson, you followed me home

forced your lips onto mine. Waited for me for hours
while I was out, prowled the dark like a badger.

Years ago, I hoped you might pursue
with such enthusiasm. I love Tony now.

And though you look handsome standing
on my porch in the dawn, back lit, dishevelled,

you'd better take your necessities back to the druggist,
and tell your wife whatever you please.

Ring ring

All of memory spins on this point
that ring of the telephone
the breath on the other end
sharp as a cuss.

Innocence crushed itself
into the receiver, fed itself
to the line, moved peristaltic
through itself

through the wire and rotated time
and all my other knowings were
diminished
to tears and falling.

You know

He was in love with me.
He told me so on several occasions.

Just two weeks before he died
was the last time.

He'd stay a while always
wanting to talk philosophy, or free love

at all hours of the night.
One time, I thought he'd take me

right there on my front porch.
I drove him full moon wild.

Burial

Standing pigeon toed
in the pin grass
some oblique speechmaker
calls you a fine man.

What would he know
about the rush of red
that hit your cheeks when
I called you darling or worse?

Or your shovels full of grainy words
that came cascading down on me
on too few afternoons
that now seem distant and brown.

Epilogue

Night table

three hand-written poems

sheets of blank paper

an electric lamp tailed by a frayed cord, topped with a dust-
laden brown shade

his Waterman pen smudged with an ink-black thumbprint

silver-plated cufflinks scratched with wear

a hardback copy of *Ulysses* pages curled by several readings

a folded page titled Yeats, reading:

*tread softly, tread softly, tread softly, tread softly, tread softly,
tread softly, tread softly, tread softly, tread softly*

Believe

this is the way the day unfurled.

The afternoon is calm as a morphine sleep.
The horizon line clear and far away. He slips
over the side into the cave of dreamers.
Into the muck he dives, unroiling the dark
with his unmoving feet, turning circles
in the depth and calling.

The boat drifts away.
Consciousness skims
across the green mirrored surface.